Leisure Arts 18

Still Life in Pastel

Aubrey Sykes

SEARCH PRESS

Wellwood North Farm Road Tunbridge Wells

Introduction

This book is primarily concerned with the use of pastel in portraying still life, but I wish to emphasise also the importance of still-life painting in general.

One of the great advantages of still life is that most of the subjects can be found in our own homes. They do not move about as in life drawing, nor are we dependent on the vagaries of the weather, as in landscape painting; so the artist has the opportunity of observing and portraying them without disturbance.

In still life, articles are in close proximity to each other. Separating them in depth, or recession, requires therefore keen observation and executive ability to render a convincing impression. Understanding tone in relation to colour is also vital.

The most successful still-life groups are usually those we 'see' as against those which are 'arranged': the coat casually thrown down on a chair; the shoes kicked off at random, and (for when one is more accomplished) interiors with their intriguing corners, angles and interplay of light and shade. Composition, of course, plays a great part in the rendering of a group, one of the difficulties being space which is limited by the size and shape of the paper we are using as a ground. All these points will, I hope, be made clearer in the pages which follow and increase your enjoyment of this particular art form.

Materials

A great advantage of pastel as a medium is that delightful results are obtainable from limited resources. Satisfactory results can even be achieved by the use of monochrome only, which means tinted paper and probably three pastels – there is little more economical than that!

What you need is a large drawing board, and a good strong easel. I often use a 'sketching' easel, which leaves both my hands free and enables me to move away from my work. With this I am able to go to my subject, especially if it is something 'seen', instead of transporting the subject to the studio. Be careful always to use a dustsheet under the easel to catch the falling pastel dust; and, when you are working from a sitting position, use an apron. Keep by you a duster to wipe your hands, a wet sponge, a putty rubber, and a jar of rice flour in which to agitate pieces of dirty pastel to restore their original colour. I possess a plastic fisherman's box with many compartments. By keeping the colours segregated – reds, blues, yellows, greens etc., in their particular colour groups – I find they become much less dirty.

You will also require sheets of tinted pastel paper. There are many different kinds: from sugar paper, which is cheap, to the more expensive Canson. Tinting watercolour paper and creating one's own background is a valuable method which I often use, but make sure you allow the paper to dry thoroughly before using the pastel. The most important factor is the 'tooth', or degree of surface roughness. In general, the smoother the ground the less grip you will get for the chalk and the less superimposing of colours is possible, since it is the 'tooth' which holds and retains the pigment. The examples in this book are worked on Canson paper of various tints.

Charcoal is essential. It mixes and blends admirably with pastel, and on its own is capable of rendering delightful tonal pictures.

Finally the pastels themselves. Do not be tempted to buy too many at the outset. You must start, of course, with a nucleus – I suggest the 'beginner's' boxes which

Colour

Begin your experiments by using pastels on white paper, for this shows the unadulterated colours and their mixes. Then try the same pastels on a variety of coloured papers, using similar pressures, and notice how different the effects are.

The examples on page 4 are obtained by using a portion of pastel on its side. (This is, incidentally, the quickest method of covering the ground; also it provides a sharp edge which is useful for drawing lines and accents.) Continue to experiment by gently rubbing the edge of the solid colour sample into the paper with your thumb or little finger; much can be learned by doodling on various grounds. Place another opaque colour on the paper, together with one equally strong alongside and gently merge the two edges together. Using black and colours in the dark strength, try intensifying the tones, bearing in mind that manufacturers only add black to darken and white to lighten their pastel tints.

On page 5 I show the swatches of colours used in three of the demonstrations in this book, so that you can compare the identical colours when applied to a variety of tinted grounds. As there is an amazing *apparent* change, it is wise to have a test strip of similarly tinted paper to the one on which you are working, in order to find the requisite pastel colour for the job. Because of this change one cannot recommend a specific range of colours without knowing the particular group being painted and on what ground. You must, however, have reds and browns for warm colours, blues and purples for cool effects, and yellows and whites for a bright range. Black and grey are essential for the darks and for general tone but, again, all are affected by the ground: the ground colour penetrates the pastel because of lightness of application, creating a change; at other times it is proximity which causes two colours to affect each other.

The swatches on page 5 are of colours used in the following demonstrations: 'A' – JUG AND FRUIT (pages 28–29); 'B' – INTERIOR (pages 24–25); 'C' – BOTTLES (pages 16–17). Compare the apparent changes caused by the ground papers. It is instructive.

contain about twelve colours. Then build up your set with small additions, when required, by selecting from the retailer's trays.

Over the years I have accumulated a large stock of colours from various manufacturers, but in general I use soft pastels supplemented by a few harder varieties for accentuating drawings. If a particular colour or tint is not available I use the nearest match and incorporate it into my colour scheme; provided the tone is not upset no one will be any the wiser once the subject has been painted.

To suggest a comprehensive list of colours is virtually impossible, for there are literally hundreds, and the colour scheme for each painting will vary considerably according to subject-matter and the tint of paper used for the support. Many colours may be blended by rubbing, although I prefer the terms 'adjustment' or 'merging', for the simple superimposing of one colour upon another on the art work will blend or change the appearance of most tints without the need to rub. Tints of a particular colour are known by a number. Find the precise tint you require and make a note of the colour and tint number for reordering.

Keep your requirements simple. Do not be tempted into purchasing unnecessary equipment.

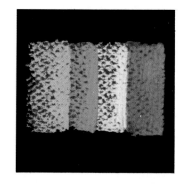

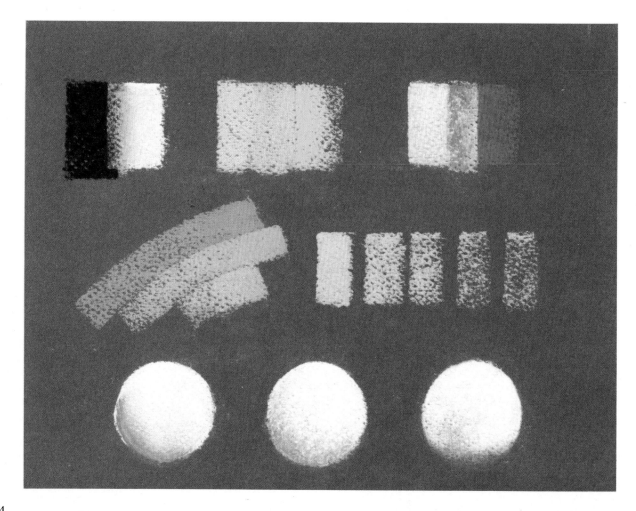

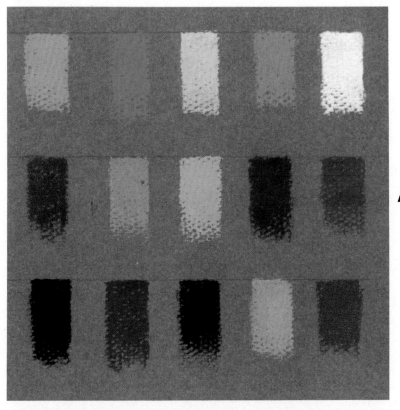

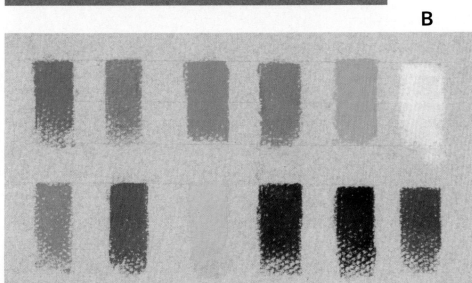

A

B

C

5

Textures

By applying the medium in different ways a variety of textures is obtained and character given to the painting. You may use all of these methods (shown here) or the particular one which you find most suitable to your own requirements, singly or together.

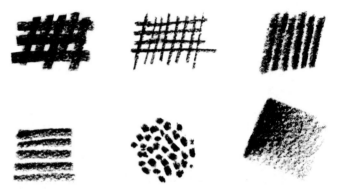

Cross-hatching is rather like the warp and weft threads in a piece of material; the more coarse the line you use the rougher the result will be. Then there are lines adjacent to each other or in juxtaposition, both vertical and horizontal, giving a very different effect. The end of the pastel or the broad side may be used, to produce a finer or a coarser line.

Pointillism, the placing of coloured dots against each other, relies on distance from your drawing to produce the desired effect.

Lastly there is the rubbing technique, which makes use of the grain of the paper. This method is almost a painting approach as opposed to the former styles which are allied more to drawing.

Some objects may be better described in a certain way. For instance, stone jars, plates, cups and saucers, all being solids, respond better to the rubbing method, with perhaps a little line work superimposed. On the other hand, cloth and other materials are better when a less opaque and a more open technique is called for, except in the highlights. In fact the high-lighted area of any subject is best treated in a much more opaque way than the shadow portion. To obtain this opacity we either rub or press very hard on the pastel.

The roughness or 'tooth' of a paper also creates texture as in the half-tone below. Renoir even used canvas as a ground, while some artists use sandpaper.

Common objects: demonstration

The objects we see around us every day form the basis of a large proportion of still-life subjects.

Before we can think in terms of a group it is necessary to draw objects individually. Each object has its own shape, colour and tone. To be able to sit in the comfort of one's own home and concentrate on a single item, without taking too much notice of adjacent impedimenta, can help the beginner who is trying to master the art of pastel.

Having studied and painted these forms separately, you have, of course, the problem of binding them together to form an artistic group, which involves composition (see page 10). For the moment, let us examine, in detail, the individual items concerned.

Generally speaking, there are three main groups: the *Opaque* such as plates, cups and saucers, jugs, wooden objects, etc.; the *Transparent*, such as bottles, glass vases, in fact anything made with glass; and lastly, *Metal* objects, which reflect light, such as the copper milk can and small cream jug in the illustrations (pages 8–9).

Most of the objects are affected to quite an extent by the colour of the ground or support upon which they are placed. The two grey papers used in the examples on pages 8–9 influence considerably the overall colour of the various items, which had been placed on similar sheets of Canson paper before the painting was begun.

The main influence of the background colour is in the shadows and half-tones where the pigment is less opaque, allowing the background colour to filter through. Wherever, such as in the lighter portions, heavy pressure on the pastel stick is used, the influence of the paper is less marked, only a comparative change is obtained by virtue of the close proximity of object to background.

Very heavy application of pigment is known as *Opaque* colour, and lighter, more delicate pressure will produce what is known as *Transparent colour* because other colour is not completely masked when superimposed. Pastel is anything but transparent in the true sense of the word. Some artists use the transparent method extensively, while others prefer the opaque method of painting throughout. I prefer a combination of both, which adds variety to the final result. So, as a general rule, I apply opaque lights and transparent darks. However, do not follow this rule slavishly – remember it is your own personal style which matters eventually.

Try using pastel for practising drawing on various coloured supports instead of always drawing with a pencil.

Do not worry if you break your pastels in the process of drawing. At my first job in a studio, using a drawing pen for some line work the studio manager, after looking at my effort, said 'break a few nibs – you'll feel more at home.' I got the message; one can be too careful!

Some of the objects depicted on pages 8–9 have had an accessory added such as the spoon on the plate and the cloth with the casserole. These help to extend the information and interest in preparation for the completion of a group.

The domestic objects which I have illustrated are essentially individual studies of each of them and in no way constitute a whole picture. They were chosen at random from around the house, and show the variety of materials and textures available in anyone's home.

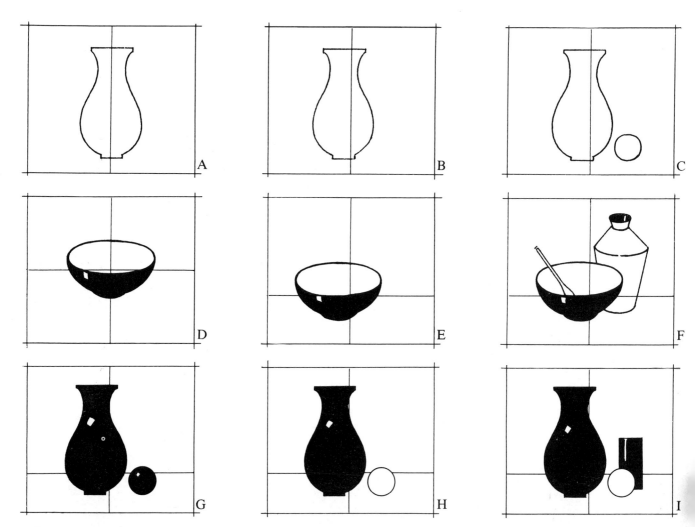

Composition

'Composition' and 'perspective' are arguably the two most daunting words in the artistic vocabulary. Many of us are unable to compose a satisfactory picture either because someone has told us we cannot, or because we are unable to bring ourselves to reposition something which we have drawn with love and care. Before you start, therefore, check the balance of your subject, whether it looks comfortably placed or not. If the first lines on your paper look aii right the composition will

not be far wrong; but if it looks awkward it must be redrawn and repositioned before you continue with the painting. No amount of colour or clever technique is going to disguise a bad composition.

The shape of the paper on which we work affects the arrangement of a group enormously, but whatever the shape or size the placing of a dominant or important object exactly centre will always look awkward and uninteresting as at (A) above. This divides the background into two identical areas, not as interesting to look at as two dissimilar shapes. From this we may deduce that similarity of shapes, lines, tones or colours will tend to produce a feeling of monotony.

The diagrams illustrate these points:–

Although the composition has been helped by placing the vase to one side (B), a smaller object or foil, the ball, has been introduced to counterbalance the vase to the left (C). In position (D) moving the horizontal lower and (E) the dish to the left has achieved a decided improvement. Including the milk can on the right and the line of the spoon on the left (F), now gives the overall appearance a comfortable balance.

Composition is not solely concerned with the linear aspect; tone, or the weight of the tone distributed throughout the picture, has a considerable bearing. The placing of these 'weights' happily within the picture area is a skill acquired, perhaps, more by experience than by any particular set of rules. However, the word 'balance' implies a situation where the secondary object merely anchors the dominant feature and prevents it from being overweighted in the other direction.

While equal areas often appear monotonous in juxtaposition, tone seems to exaggerate this. By placing one object against another of similar tone, the overall harmony or balance is disturbed. In (G) the tonal weight of the vase is projected into the right-hand half of the paper by means of the black ball and there is a feeling of balance, but this is not so in (H) where the tone has been removed from the ball, throwing the picture balance back again to the left. The harmony is again restored in (I) by the introduction of the small black vase to the right. In a group these secondary objects must not compete with the main motif, which here is the large vase; they are complementary and must remain subservient. There should be only one dominant feature in a composition (but remember that these 'rules' are not infallible, and are not to be followed slavishly).

In the kitchen: demonstration

This still-life painting arose when I saw my wife busy in the kitchen one morning (but I rearranged it when I had the kitchen to myself!). It was, however, painted on the spot and not in the studio. (Do not forget the dust-sheet on the floor!)

Stage 1 (page 12)

I draw in the lines of the composition in charcoal on a buff paper, creating a division of the area into pleasing shapes. This helps the general balance while the lines themselves give direction and movement. This 'linear' composition is a sketching-in of the main structure of the picture.

Stage 2

The main addition here is tone, not too heavy at this stage, but notice how this enhances the composition and begins to establish a more solid and balanced appearance. I use a sepia pastel as being the best way to establish greater strength as soon as possible.

Stage 3

The light colour and white of the tea cloth are next introduced, together with suggestions of the actual local colour of the various objects. We now see, having placed the whites of the cloth and the flour, how strong is the tone of the buff ground. The sooner I recognise this the sooner I can adjust the general tones of the picture. The buff ground was chosen as being the most helpful in this particular instance and it becomes more apparent as the picture develops.

Stage 1

Stage 2

Stage 3

Stage 4

The local colour on the jug, lemon, mixing bowl etc. is only generally indicated at this stage but it gives a good idea of how the eventual picture will look.

Stage 4

More local colour is added with highlight accents at various points. I then work over the whole area bringing up to strength the half-tones and intermediate colours. This becomes a much easier process as I have already established the darkest darks and the lightest lights as minimum and maximum strengths.

Stage 5 – the finished painting

Much of the final painting concerns detail, and this has to be approached with restraint. It is not only tempting to smooth over the half-tones but tempting also to over-

Stage 5 – the finished painting

state the amount of detail included. A certain amount of drawing needs to be emphasised, and a little more careful rubbing with the finger to fuse various passages of colour will be necessary, as well as softening some edges and, lastly, adding the highlights.

If you have over-worked any part of the painting surface, brush it out with a hog-hair brush and start again. You cannot apply subtle drawing and fine detail on heavily applied pigment.

I have included a colour swatch with the finished picture as it progressed, having purposely omitted the tint names and numbers.

See also detail, page 32.

Finish

The word 'finish' usually refers to the degree of attention given to the actual working of the pastel in its final stages, such as the amount of softening of edges and the subscribing to detail (or over-subscribing as the case may be). Strictly speaking, the amount of 'work' is deemed sufficient depending on how far the artist wishes to take the final stage of the painting. It is unwise to over-indulge in detail or the process of softening until one has the necessary discipline and restraint in one's armoury, like the Dutch masters who knew how to prevent any detail spoiling the unity of the whole picture.

If only a sketch is required then you complete or finish it at an early stage, often necessary for lack of time or the need to obtain an effect quickly, for example, fleeting light. A thorough examination of the subject will require more detail – more tones and colours, more variety of planes – in fact the more we do, the more 'finish' we are adding to our painting and it becomes, progressively, more subtle and difficult. It is easy to over-work a pastel but it is just as easy to underwork one. The underworked pastel is usually very thin, relying, as it does, on understatement and slickness; an over-worked one, on the other hand, becomes a 'pudding' and so loses all character. Something between the two, therefore, is the result to aim for. Sufficient tooth must be retained in the paper to enable the final work you apply to be superimposed in the final operation. The rule here is 'Don't rub in too much thickness of pastel in the early stages', never lose the tooth or grain of the paper until the final accents and highlights. Should it become overloaded with pigment, as can happen, dust off the surplus with a hog-hair brush and redraw the offending passage, only this time be more careful! Luckily, the pastel medium is an accommodating one.

The contrast between a rough finished pastel (above) *and a smooth finished painting* (below).

Bottles: demonstration

Bottles, individually and collectively, contain rich colours, the strange distorted shapes seen through them are always fascinating, and portraying transparent glass and its reflecting surfaces is a challenge to the artist.

The paper colour for your pastel picture depends very much on the contrast you require for the lights coming through the bottles. It should not be too pale but, apart from that, choose the colour you feel goes with the group. If you place an identical piece of paper behind the still-life group itself, this will indicate the correct relationship between the various tones and colours of the pastel sticks you use.

Stage 1 (page 16)

The drawing stage is completed and a certain amount of dark colour is drawn lightly across the paper – rather feeling my way. I had decided that the group looked more interesting if I took the neck of the champagne bottle above and out of the picture area, and allowed the rest of the group to be drawn that much larger.

Stage 2

I next produce a strong emphasis on darks which is desirable because of the intense depth of tone in each of the bottles. I place the darks first, for then I know the absolute or maximum depth of tone available to me.

Stage 3

I next establish the lightest tone, which is the napkin. I now have the maximum and minimum of dark and light; all that is required is the painting of the areas between these two extremes. Painting in the white napkin at this stage also gives me the true value of the background tone. As it will have a considerable influence on the final result, I state it as soon as possible.

The build-up of the picture must be gradual to avoid mistakes. If one does occur and, after brushing out, a return to beginnings is desired this may be completed by the gentle application of a putty rubber, but only *after* the brush has taken off all the surplus pigment.

Stage 4

Further half-tones, details and highlights build up towards the final stage. By drawing with dark colours I emphasise the strange shapes seen in the bottles.

Stage 5 – the finished painting

A certain amount of rubbing or adjusting the contours and edges is needed before finally placing the detailed highlights. I add the background, draw in the labels and give more form to the napkin.

Have you noticed the usefulness of the green line on the napkin? Apart from their decorative value, stripes are useful to describe contours. Converging lines also aid the feeling of recession and give depth to a picture.

Stage 1

Stage 2

Stage 3

Stage 4

Stage 5 – the finished painting

The seeing eye

The still life 'seen' may be better than the one 'arranged', but this needs some explanation, for it is truer to say that the still life 'seen' is better than the *badly* arranged group. There are certain indefinable qualities in a 'seen' still life which you cannot reproduce by arranging a group however hard you try. I admit, many masterpieces exist of arranged groups but to my mind they do not compare with an inspired reaction to the appearance of something seen: something which does not require adjustment. You have only to look around your own home to see what I mean.

The casual throwing of a coat over a chair, the collection of items on a kitchen draining board, children's toys left abandoned, all these are there to be observed before one tidies the place. I am not suggesting that you become untidy, but do look around before disturbing something that could eventually be the inspiration for a picture – and, what is more, do not just look: do something about it! Many of the paintings of Van Gogh and Cezanne were of something seen rather than arranged, even though both painters did not hesitate to make adjustments to their pictures if they felt it necessary. It is however, the experience of arranging which educates the eye to see the beauty which is around us, so do not hesitate to spend time re-arranging a still life: it will not prove wasted effort.

We have to cultivate a 'seeing' eye by knowing what to look for. This can only be achieved by practice. The trained eye is always looking and comparing one thing against another. Using a sketch book is the best method of remembering what we have observed.

A successful still life need not have for its main interest a valuable ornament. A beautiful ornament will not necessarily make a beautiful picture. We are dealing with shapes, tones and colours placed within an existing area, and these conditions are just as important,

whether we are dealing with *objets d'art* or a collection of old boots lying around the house.

Often a particular light governs whether we like a setting or not; sometimes a change of light will create the requisite conditions for an interesting painting from the most ordinary of subjects. The play of light coming through a window or an open door at certain times of the day is sufficient to stimulate interest to the least experienced eye, and perhaps the desire to paint.

Children's toys

As subject-matter for still life, children's toys can be most exciting, for the simple colours and shapes offer many possibilities. Dolls, in particular, are excellent material, as are puppets. A friend of mine, many years ago, specialised in still life with puppets, for he found that they added drama to a still-life subject.

Toys are most effective for picture-making when they are found precisely as the children have left them, lying around in an untidy but spontaneous jumble. The examples shown on the following pages were borrowed from a neighbour with a young family. They in no way constitute a picture, for I merely drew them as individual items out of interest, and to show the variety of objects that might engage your interest when deciding what to look for in composing a still life.

Viewpoints

Still life is not always a group of objects situated just below eye level on a flat foreground at right angles to an upright plane. There are many other viewpoints and interesting angles to explore.

Look at objects on a low window ledge, a high shelf, or even on the floor. The lower or higher the viewpoint the more difficult is the drawing of the ellipses or ovals. When the ellipse approaches the full circle, any bad drawing shows immediately; and when the perspective, which in these instances can be very subtle indeed, is not properly described, the whole effort becomes a disaster. But do not allow this to put you off or send you back to the simpler but less interesting eye-level rendering. It is a question of drawing and perseverence.

This is one of the reasons why I recommend drawing at all times from whatever angle you may happen to see your subject. The objects themselves may not form any sort of picture or make a composition, but the eye and hand become more accustomed to dealing with an unusual viewpoint, thus adding considerably to the variety and interest of your still-life subjects.

The accepted format of foreground and background being separate is not always the case; they are often one unit, such as when a group is on the floor, which then becomes foreground and background together. Of course the tone will vary from front to back but it will still be one item.

Objects seen on a table are often made more interesting by using the perspective angle of the table itself and by including, in a very low key, the furniture beyond the actual group as in the demonstration 'In the kitchen' (pages 12–13). Putting a tea cloth or napkin with your group enlivens, as does a drape on the background, the softness and change of texture which is so helpful as a contrast to the rigid and harder appearance of the common objects. A cup or container on its side

Looking down on objects can give them a more interesting perspective.

(not easy to draw), a lid perhaps set against the upright side of a jar, will introduce new and attractive variants to the composition, all contributing to the variety and overall success of the picture.

Interior: demonstration

An interior is usually a collection of still-life objects but involving more perspective as well as composition. This subject was 'seen', as are most interiors, and not arranged.

The light coming through a window or doorway often provides an interesting and exciting subject for painting. I have painted many interior subjects, sometimes including my wife as a solitary figure carrying our some domestic chore, but I prefer the figure, if used, to be secondary in importance, otherwise the picture ceases to be an interior and becomes a portrait with an interior background. The straightforward presentation of an interior with its interesting angles and planes, however, together with an exciting light pattern, can convey a mood or a story without the addition of a human figure.

Stage 1 (page 24)

I draw in the outlines with charcoal, making sure that there is a possible composition and that I have included the main points of interest which first attracted me to the subject.

Stage 2

This stage is supplemented by the careful addition of darks and half-tones – a tonal sketch, in fact.

Stage 3

The main light in the picture appears on the curtains, the glazing bars of the window, and on the lawn seen through the window. I have tried to keep the lawn the principal light area: this means that the others have to be modified to some extent.

There are two ways of doing this – one is to mute the not-so-important lights; the other is to place a dark or dark half-tone against the dominant light area to dramatise it. A little of each method is adopted here as a sort of compromise. As a general rule, it is important to decide which is the dominant light and to make sure that the others give way in order of tonal value.

Stage 4

Placing the dark tone of the bush against the light on the lawn is helpful, but further toning down of the glazing bars is necessary to give recession through the window to the garden beyond. Introducing detail proves difficult, for the temptation to over-subscribe could lead to a loss of unity over the whole picture. Detail we must have, but it must not be too assertive.

Stage 5 – the finished painting

With the final drawing-in, I use a fairly sharp edge on the pastel for the finer lines and detail. This can be obtained by using the edge of a broken stick of colour or by fining down an existing piece by rubbing it on a rough paper. If a large amount of your pastel stick has to be removed, use a sheet of glass paper, then finish off with rough paper.

Many of the darker areas and items I now adjust by introducing a slightly different colour to provide variety, to relieve the monotony of the darks, and produce a more acceptable colour harmony. This introduced colour need not be a reduction of the tone already there, but is invariably a change of colour caused by reflected light in the darks from other objects. The selection of the right colour and tone comes with experience; but aim to balance both tones and hues (the strength of a colour) so that your finished picture has unity.

Stage 1

Stage 2

Stage 3

Stage 4

Stage 5 – the finished painting

Tone

We can obtain a better idea of tone if we paint in monochrome without any reference to colour. Just paint the tones or describe the forms – in fact, make a picture similar to a black and white photograph. Tone is a basic requirement in all painting, colour is merely an extension of this element. Together, they produce a complete interpretation of a subject. However, painting a good monochrome can be most satisfying in itself.

The introduction of colour must be made without upsetting the tone values already established. Also, do not forget that colours have their own individual and varied tone values. The similarity of tones in red and green colour-blindness test-cards causes the most confusion, because in them the tones are so similar in strength. However, if one of them is a very light green, and the other a very dark red, the difference is easily distinguished. This example illustrates how the actual *tones* of colours can upset the balance of a monochrome painting unless we take great care. If two similar 'colour tone' objects are placed together, they seem to flatten or merge and their individual importance is affected. As far as the composition is concerned, they become, in weight, one object. Sometimes this is an advantage but we must intend it to be so.

Colour and interpreting it is mainly a matter of temperament; but all interpretations are subject to tone values.

Jug and fruit: demonstration

This painting is different in style to the previous examples and illustrates the point that there is no right or wrong way to apply the pastel.

I chose the dark blue-grey paper in order to make full use of this colour in the various objects composing the group. I made extensive use of it also in the background, in the tray, and within the shadows generally. It also gives me the necessary contrasting tone with which to obtain the brilliance of colour on the fruit.

Stage 1 (page 28)

I draw in the picture using white, but any light neutral colour would have suited just as well. The group is simple and I move it around until a satisfactory arrangement is achieved.

Stage 2

Having decided the general composition, I place a few strokes of colour around to emphasise the shapes and indicate the tonal values: these are only approximate.

Stage 3

As you see, all these strokes are made by the broadside of a piece of pastel and are not rubbed in. The only blending together of pigment is produced by the superimposing of one colour on another, thereby obtaining the desired effect. This broad stylised technique has to be maintained throughout if continuity is to be preserved. Tempting though it is to rub with your finger or thumb – please do not.

Neutral colours, such as black or vandyke brown with white on grey or brown paper, are admirable for making studies in monochrome. I have adopted this technique at the first stages of the demonstrations in this book. As you become more experienced in handling pastels you will find it is not necessary to pursue the tonal effect to its ultimate state before introducing colour.

Stage 1

Stage 2

Stage 3

Stage 4

Stage 4

Another factor is the firm direction of the strokes I use, which do not always follow the recognised form of the object. Sometimes the direction appears to be going 'against the grain' instead of with it. The general result is a patchwork of colours or mosaics. This can be seen clearly in the build-up to the final picture.

There is a certain vigour about this method of painting with pastel, but one must not get too stylised and sacrifice sound workmanship for technique – one of the pitfalls in the use of pastel which we all blunder into

from time to time. But neither should experiment be discouraged, so try something a little different occasionally.

When using this treatment it is preferable to make short strokes only and vary the direction as much as possible.

Stage 5 – the finished painting

In the final painting I endeavour to minimise the exaggerated effect by cross-hatching with other strokes in a different direction, softening the overall appearance and making the final result more pleasing.

Stage 5 – the finished painting

Where the background paper colour is used extensively in the design, great care must be exercised in the application of the pastel. Make sure that not all of the ground colour is eliminated, otherwise the effort of choosing a particular paper will have been wasted and the advantages lost. The paper colour will show through in the half-tones and darks where the pigment is not so heavy. Obviously where the colour requires extreme pressure, as in the highlights and lighter portions, none or very little of this ground will penetrate.

By experimenting you will learn a great deal about the use of pastel and eventually obtain a technique of your own. But one warning; do not aim at style. Painting techniques are a means to an end; when we become practised in the medium it is better to concentrate on the subject-matter – style will follow. Then your paintings will acquire their own particular individuality.

Drawing and observation

Drawing and observation constitute the foundation of an artist's training. It is not sufficient just to look at something: we must observe, analyse, then record by drawing. The one helps the other, the co-ordination between hand and eye being essential for good drawing or painting.

To draw, we have to analyse the subject in front of us. This in turn is impressed on our mind, which then motivates the hand to make the necessary strokes on the paper. Even a few lines in a sketch book can convey more to the artist and be remembered longer than numerous photographs. For, by drawing, we are forced to take notice and memorise. Drawing is also the discipline of painting; unless the hand and eye are drilled and co-ordinated, how can we record our impressions successfully?

There is no exclusive or right way to draw. Each person develops his or her own style. Every style is acceptable and each expresses the subject in a personal way. What is important is that the result be an honest rendering of the subject-matter and not just an effort to impress by dexterity or slickness.

Keep a sketch book handy and use it as often as possible; even making a few sketchy lines gets one into the habit of drawing. However, it is important from time to time to make more careful studies and to carry sketches beyond the brief statement to a more informed and detailed drawing. To become accustomed to the sketched impression limits the ability to progress and develop.

When drawing more than one object, consider the relationship between the various items chosen. Drawing a collection of items, as against single specimens, teaches us the rudiments of the all-important art of picture-making; in other words, composition. Give the group a limit by surrounding the items with a border, otherwise the tendency is to go on adding items *ad infinitum* until your composition becomes completely lost.

At times, however, I do add to a still-life group, even after beginning the actual picture, if the overall design seems to demand it. It is the final effect which matters.

This book has not dealt with the painting of flowers as such, but their use as an accessory can enhance a still-life group.

The preliminary sketch (*left*) was made prior to the painting of a finished picture. It illustrates the added interest flowers can contribute to the overall effect. When flowers are used in conjunction with common objects, I find it is better not to overload the picture with them; great bunches of flowers are difficult to portray, anyway, and often lead to a feeling of disappointment when the picture is finished.

ACKNOWLEDGEMENTS

Text, drawings and paintings by Aubrey Sykes

First published in Great Britain in 1983 by Search Press Limited, Wellwood, North Farm Road, Tunbridge Wells, Kent TN2 3DR

Text, illustrations, arrangement and typography copyright © Search Press Limited 1983.

Reprinted 1989

U.S. Artists Materials Trade Distributor:
Winsor & Newton, Inc.
P. O. Box 1519, 555 Winsor Drive, Secaucus, NJ 07094

Canadian Distributors:
Anthes Universal Limited
341 Heart Lake Road South, Brampton, Ontario L6W 3K8

Australian Distributors:
Jasco Pty. Limited
937-941 Victoria Road, West Ryde, N.S.W. 2114

New Zealand Distributors:
Caldwell Wholesale Ltd
Wellington and Auckland

ISBN 0 85532 525 9

Made and printed in Spain by Artes Graphicas Elkar, S. Coop. Autonomía, 71 - 48012-Bilbao - Spain.

Detail from 'In the kitchen' demonstration, pages 11–13.